PRINCIPLES FOR BUILDING WEALTH, AVOIDING DEBT, AND ACHIEVING FINANCIAL FREEDOM

BIBLICAL WISDOM. SMART STRATEGIES.
A LEGACY THAT LASTS GENERATIONS.

MANAGE GOD'S RESOURCES WISELY.
BUILD WEALTH FAITHFULLY. LIVE FREELY.

VAUGHN & YOLANDA COWAN

FAITHFUL SERVANTS. FINANCIAL EDUCATORS. LEGACY BUILDERS.

Unless otherwise indicated, scriptures are taken from several version of the Bible (NIV) (KVJ) (MSG)(ESV)

IBSN: 9780960108176

Principles for Building Wealth, Avoiding Debt, and Achieving Financial Freedom

Biblical Wisdom, Smart Strategies, A legacy that lasts generations.

Authors: Vaughn and Yolanda Cowan

Published by
Printed in the United States
First Edition: August 2026

Table of Contents

Introduction
Wealth Is More Than Money

"The earth is the Lord's, and everything in it, the world, and all who live in it." — Psalm 24:1

Money is one of the most important resources God places in our hands. It can provide security, create opportunities, support our families, and enable us to bless others. Yet for many people, money is also a source of stress, worry, and uncertainty.

The truth is, financial freedom is not determined by how much money you earn. Every year, people with high incomes find themselves overwhelmed by debt, while others with modest incomes quietly build wealth through discipline, wise decisions, and consistent stewardship.

The difference is not income it is behavior.

Throughout our lives, we have discovered that lasting financial freedom requires both biblical wisdom and practical financial knowledge.

As a teacher of Biblical Financial Freedom, Vaughn has spent years helping individuals understand God's principles of stewardship. His passion is to show that everything we have belongs to God, and we are called to manage His blessings with faithfulness, wisdom, and integrity.

As an Enrolled Agent, tax strategist, business owner, and financial educator, I have worked with thousands of individuals, families, and business owners. One lesson has become clear: earning more money does not automatically create wealth. Financial success comes from making wise decisions with the resources you already have.

This book brings those two perspectives together.

Part I focuses on the biblical principles that build a strong financial foundation. Part II provides practical strategies for budgeting, investing, tax planning, wealth building, and creating a financial legacy.

Our goal is not simply to help you earn more money. Our goal is to help you become a faithful steward, eliminate unnecessary debt, build lasting wealth, and experience the freedom that comes from managing your finances with purpose.

One principle guides this entire book:

If you don't learn how to make money while you sleep, you will spend your life working for money instead of allowing your money to work for you.

Financial freedom does not happen overnight. It is built one wise decision at a time. Every dollar you save, every debt you eliminate, every investment you make, and every act of faithful stewardship moves you one step closer to the future you desire.

As you read, we encourage you to reflect on your own financial habits and apply the principles in each chapter. Small, consistent changes often produce extraordinary results over time.

Whether you are just beginning your financial journey or looking to strengthen the foundation you have already built, we pray this book equips and encourages you to honor God with your finances, provide for your family, and build a legacy that will bless generations to come.

Welcome to your journey toward Biblical Financial Freedom

Chapter 1
Zero-Balance Thinking
If You Can't Afford It, Don't Buy It

"The rich rule over the poor, and the borrower is servant to the lender."— **Proverbs 22:7 (NIV)**

Vaughn and Yolanda's Principle

"Financial freedom begins the moment you faithfully manage what God has already placed in your hands."

God calls us to be faithful stewards, not careless consumers. Before we ask God for more, we should learn to wisely manage what we already have. The habits we develop today determine the opportunities we are prepared to receive tomorrow.

Stewardship Starts with Everyday Decisions

Many people believe financial freedom begins with earning more money. While increasing your income can improve your financial situation, income alone does not create wealth. The true foundation of financial freedom is wise stewardship.

Stewardship means responsibly managing the resources God has entrusted to us. Every dollar we earn presents a choice. We can either spend it impulsively or use it intentionally to provide for our families, prepare for the future, and honor God.

One of the greatest financial mistakes people make is spending money they do not have. Our culture constantly encourages instant gratification. Advertisements tell us we deserve the newest car, the latest phone, larger homes, and luxury vacations. Credit is readily available, making it easy to purchase today and worry about the payment later.

However, every unnecessary payment limit future opportunity. Monthly debt obligations reduce your ability to save, invest, give generously, and prepare for unexpected emergencies.

Zero-Balance Thinking challenges us to think differently.

Instead of asking, *"Can I afford the monthly payment?"* ask, *"Can I truly afford this purchase?"*

If buying something requires unnecessary debt, it may not be the right time to buy it.

Needs, Wants, and Wisdom

Wise financial decisions begin by understanding the difference between needs and wants.

Needs include food, shelter, clothing, transportation, healthcare, and other basic necessities.

Wants are things that improve our comfort or enjoyment but are not essential.

There is nothing wrong with enjoying God's blessings. The problem begins when wants become more important than financial stability. Many people borrow money to purchase things that lose value almost immediately, leaving them with years of payments for something that no longer brings lasting satisfaction.

Contentment helps us avoid this trap. When we appreciate what God has already provided, we become less driven by comparison and impulse.

Five Questions Before Every Purchase

Before making any significant purchase, ask yourself:

- Do I really need this?

- Can I pay cash for it?
- Will this purchase improve my financial future?
- Am I buying this because of emotion or wisdom?
- Will I still be happy with this purchase a year from now?

These simple questions can prevent many costly financial mistakes.

Kingdom Challenge

For the next 30 days, delay every non-essential purchase for at least 24 hours.

Use that time to pray, review your budget, and consider whether the purchase supports your long-term financial goals.

If you decide not to make the purchase, transfer that money into savings or an investment account.

Small decisions repeated consistently produce lasting financial freedom.

Reflection Questions

- Where do I struggle most with impulse spending?
- Have I confused wants with needs?
- What financial habit do I need to change this month?
- How can I become a better steward of God's resources?

Biblical Wisdom

"Whoever can be trusted with very little can also be trusted with much." — Luke 16:10 (NIV)

Faithfulness with today's resources prepares us for tomorrow's opportunities.

Notes:

Chapter 2
Build an Emergency Fund
Save Before You Spend

*"The wise store up choice food and olive oil, but fools gulp theirs down."— **Proverbs 21:20 (NIV)***

Vaughn and Yolanda's Principle

"An emergency fund is more than money in the bank it is a reflection of wisdom, preparation, and faithful stewardship."

Preparing for tomorrow is not a lack of faith; it is an act of wisdom. God calls us to be responsible stewards by planning ahead and managing our resources wisely. An emergency fund helps us face life's unexpected challenges without allowing them to become financial crises.

Expect the Unexpected

- Life is full of surprises.
- Your car may need unexpected repairs.
- A family member may face a medical emergency.
- Your water heater could stop working.
- A storm may damage your home.

You could experience a job loss or a reduction in income.

None of these situations are planned, yet they happen to nearly everyone. The question is not if an emergency will occur it is when.

Without savings, many people are forced to rely on credit cards, personal loans, or borrowing from family and friends.

What begins as a temporary problem often turns into long-term debt.

An emergency fund gives you options. Instead of reacting in fear, you can respond with confidence because you have prepared in advance.

Saving Is an Act of Wisdom

Some people believe that saving money shows a lack of faith in God. The Bible teaches otherwise.

Throughout Scripture, we see examples of wise planning and preparation. God calls us to trust Him while also being responsible stewards of the resources He provides.

Saving money is not expecting the worst—it is preparing wisely for life's realities.

Just as we purchase insurance hoping we never need it, an emergency fund provides peace of mind while protecting our financial future.

Start Small, Stay Consistent

Many people never begin saving because they believe they need to save thousands of dollars immediately.

Don't let the size of the goal stop you from taking the first step.

Start where you are.

- Save $20.
- Then $50.
- Then $100.

Small amounts saved consistently become significant over time.

The habit of saving is more important than the amount you save in the beginning.

Every dollar you set aside today strengthens your financial future.

Build Your Emergency Fund in Stages

Building an emergency fund does not happen overnight. It is a process.

Stage One: Save your first $1,000.

This amount can often cover minor emergencies like car repairs, deductibles, or unexpected household expenses.

Stage Two: Save one month of living expenses.

This provides a stronger financial cushion and helps reduce the need to rely on credit during difficult times.

Stage Three: Build three to six months of living expenses.

This level of savings can provide security during a job loss, illness, or other major life event.

Each stage moves you closer to financial stability and peace of mind.

Pay Yourself First

One of the most effective financial habits is paying yourself first.

Before paying discretionary expenses, set aside a portion of every paycheck for savings.

Treat your savings as a priority rather than an afterthought.

Even if you begin with only five or ten percent of your income, consistency matters more than perfection.

Automating your savings can make this habit even easier. When money is transferred into savings before you have the opportunity to spend it, saving becomes part of your routine instead of a monthly struggle.

Avoid Common Mistakes

Building an emergency fund requires discipline.

Avoid these common mistakes:

- Using your emergency fund for vacations or entertainment.
- Spending your savings on impulse purchases.
- Failing to replenish your emergency fund after using it.
- Keeping all your savings in an account that is too easy to access for unnecessary spending.

Remember, an emergency fund is reserved for genuine emergencies not convenience.

Kingdom Challenge

This week, open or designate a savings account specifically for emergencies.

Commit to saving something from every paycheck, regardless of the amount.

If you already have an emergency fund, review it and determine whether it is sufficient to cover today's living expenses.

Faithful preparation today creates greater peace tomorrow.

Reflection Questions

- If an unexpected expense occurred today, how would I pay for it?
- Am I relying on savings or credit when emergencies happen?
- What amount can I begin saving consistently?
- What changes can I make to reach my emergency savings goal more quickly?

Take a few moments to write your answers and develop a simple savings plan.

Biblical Wisdom

"The prudent see danger and take refuge, but the simple keep going and pay the penalty."— **Proverbs 22:3 (NIV)**

Wisdom prepares before problems arise. A faithful steward does not wait for a crisis before making wise financial decisions.

Notes:

Chapter 3
The Buy Five Rule
If You Can't Buy Five, Don't Buy One

*"The plans of the diligent lead to profit as surely as haste leads to poverty."— **Proverbs 21:5 (NIV)***

Vaughn and Yolanda's Principle

"Don't measure affordability by what you can borrow. Measure it by what you can comfortably own without compromising your financial future."

A Different Way to Measure Affordability

One of the biggest financial traps people fall into is believing they can afford something simply because they qualify for the monthly payment.

Car dealerships advertise monthly payments instead of the total cost. Furniture stores promise "no money down." Credit card companies encourage minimum payments, making expensive purchases seem affordable.

But making the payment and affording the purchase are not the same thing.

The Buy Five Rule offers a different way to think about spending.

If you cannot comfortably purchase five of any items with cash, you should carefully consider whether you can truly afford one.

This principle is not about buying five of everything. It is about measuring your financial capacity rather than your borrowing ability.

Think Like a Steward, not a Consumer

God calls us to manage our resources wisely. Every financial decision should reflect careful planning rather than impulsive spending.

Consumers often ask:

"Can I make the payment?"

Wise stewards ask:

"Will this purchase strengthen or weaken my financial future?"

That single question changes how we view money.

The Buy Five Rule encourages us to slow down, evaluate our priorities, and make decisions that support long-term financial freedom rather than short-term satisfaction.

Why This Rule Works

The Buy Five Rule creates healthy financial boundaries.

It helps prevent overspending.

It reduces emotional purchases.

It encourages saving before spending.

Most importantly, it reminds us that true affordability is determined by financial strength—not available credit.

For example, if you're considering purchasing a $2,000 television, ask yourself whether you could comfortably pay $10,000 in cash without affecting your emergency fund, monthly bills, or investments.

If the answer is no, it may be wise to postpone the purchase until your financial position is stronger.

Waiting is not failure. Waiting is wisdom.

Affordability Is More Than Cash

The Buy Five Rule is not about becoming wealthy enough to buy five luxury cars or five expensive watches.

It is about maintaining financial balance.

Before making a significant purchase, ask yourself:

- Will this purchase reduce my savings?
- Will it increase my debt?
- Will it prevent me from investing?
- Will it create unnecessary financial stress?
- Is this purchase a need or simply a desire?

If the purchase keeps you from meeting your financial responsibilities or reaching your long-term goals, it may not be the right time.

Practice Patience

One of the greatest financial habits you can develop is patience.

Many of the purchases we regret were made because we acted too quickly.

Give yourself time.

Save for what you want.

When you finally make the purchase, you'll enjoy it far more because it was made from a position of financial strength rather than financial pressure.

Patience protects your peace.

Stewardship Challenge

Before making your next major purchase, apply the Buy Five Rule.

Ask yourself:

- Could I comfortably purchase five of these items with cash?
- Would doing so leave my finances healthy and secure?
- If not, can I wait while I continue saving?

Write down your answers before making the purchase.

Reflection Questions

- Have I confused qualifying for credit with being able to afford something?
- What large purchase have I made that created unnecessary financial stress?
- How would applying the Buy Five Rule change my spending habits?
- What financial goal is worth waiting for?

Biblical Wisdom

"Suppose one of you wants to build a tower. Won't you first sit down and estimate the cost to see if you have enough money to complete it?"— **Luke 14:28 (NIV)**

Wise stewardship begins with careful planning. God encourages us to count the cost before making financial commitments.

Notes:

Chapter 4
Stay Away from Consumer Debt

"The rich rule over the poor, and the borrower is slave to the lender."
— Proverbs 22:7 (NIV)

Vaughn and Yolanda's Principle

"Debt should never become the master of your future. Financial freedom grows when you own your choices instead of owing for them."

Understanding the Difference

Not all debt is created equal.

Some forms of borrowing may help build wealth when approached carefully and responsibly. However, consumer debt is often used to purchase items that lose value over time while continuing to require monthly payments.

Examples include:

- Credit card balances
- Personal loans
- Buy Now, Pay Later purchases
- Furniture financing
- High-interest financing
- Payday loans

These types of debt often provide temporary satisfaction but can create long-term financial burdens.

As faithful stewards, we should carefully consider whether a purchase is worth sacrificing future income.

The High Cost of Consumer Debt

Every monthly payment reduces your ability to save, invest, give generously, and prepare for the future.

Consumer debt quietly limits your financial choices.

Instead of using your income to build wealth, you use it to repay yesterday's purchases.

Many people spend years paying for items they no longer own or use.

The excitement of the purchase fades, but the payment often remains.

Ask Before You Borrow

Before financing any purchase, ask yourself:

- Is this a necessity or simply a desire?
- Will this item increase or decrease in value?
- Can I save and purchase it later?
- Will this debt delay my financial goals?
- Does this decision reflect wise stewardship?

Sometimes the wisest financial decision is simply waiting.

Freedom Is Worth Waiting For

Our culture celebrates immediate gratification.

God teaches patience, wisdom, and self-control.

Waiting allows you to save, avoid unnecessary interest, and purchase from a position of strength rather than pressure.

Financial freedom is often built by the purchases we choose not to make.

Stewardship Challenge

Review every monthly payment you currently have.

Ask yourself:

- Which payments are building my future?
- Which payments are simply financing past decisions?

Choose one unnecessary debt and create a plan to eliminate it as quickly as possible.

Reflection Questions

- Which debts create the greatest stress in my life?
- What purchases could I have delayed?
- What debt can I begin paying off this month?
- How will becoming debt-free improve my ability to serve my family and God?

Biblical Wisdom

"Let no debt remain outstanding, except the continuing debt to love one another." — **Romans 13:8 (NIV)**

God desires that we live with integrity, wisdom, and freedom not unnecessary financial bondage.

Notes:

Chapter 5
Buy Assets, Not Liabilities
Build Wealth That Works for You

"Precious treasure and oil are in a wise man's dwelling, but a foolish man devours it."— **Proverbs 21:20 (ESV)**

Vaughn and Yolanda's Principle

"Wealth is built by acquiring assets that strengthen your future, not liabilities that consume your income."

Every Dollar Has an Assignment

Every dollar you earn has a purpose. The question is whether you are using it to build your future or simply finance your lifestyle.

One of the greatest differences between financially successful people and those who struggle financially is how they use their money. Wise stewards understand that money is a tool. Instead of spending every dollar on things that provide temporary satisfaction, they intentionally use a portion of their income to acquire assets that can grow in value or generate future income.

God has entrusted us with resources to manage wisely. As faithful stewards, we should ask ourselves whether our financial decisions are creating opportunities for tomorrow or simply satisfying today's desires.

Understanding Assets and Liabilities

An asset is something that contributes to your long-term financial well-being. Some assets increase in value over time, while others generate income or create opportunities for future financial growth.

Examples of assets include:

- Stocks and mutual funds
- Rental properties
- Businesses
- Dividend-paying investments
- Retirement accounts
- Royalties from books, music, or other intellectual property

Liabilities, on the other hand, are financial obligations that require ongoing expenses and often decrease in value over time.

Examples include:

- Luxury vehicles with large monthly payments
- Boats
- Timeshares
- Recreational vehicles
- High-interest consumer debt
- Expensive electronics financed over several years

Owning a liability is not necessarily wrong. The important question is whether it fits within your financial plan and whether it limits your ability to build wealth.

Think Beyond Today

Every purchase has a long-term impact.

Before making a major financial decision, ask yourself:

Will this purchase make me financially stronger or financially weaker five years from now?

Some purchases provide enjoyment today but create financial burdens tomorrow.

Other purchases may require patience, but they continue providing value for years to come.

Wise stewardship means looking beyond immediate satisfaction and considering the long-term impact of every financial decision.

Let Your Money Work for You

Many people spend their entire lives working for money.

The goal is to reach a point where your money begins working for you.

Assets have the potential to produce income whether you are working, traveling, spending time with your family, or sleeping.

This is one of the foundational principles of financial freedom.

Every asset you acquire becomes another opportunity for your money to grow and serve your future.

Build Before You Upgrade

Our culture encourages us to upgrade our lifestyle every time our income increases.

A promotion often leads to a newer car.

A raise becomes an excuse for a larger house.

A bonus quickly disappears on luxury purchases.

Wise stewards think differently.

Instead of immediately increasing their lifestyle, they first increase their investments. They build assets before upgrading their standard of living.

Over time, those assets begin producing income that helps pay for future wants without creating unnecessary financial pressure.

Stewardship Challenge

- Take inventory of your finances this week.
- Create two lists.
- On the first list, write every asset you own.
- On the second list, write every liability you currently pay for.

Ask yourself:

- Which assets are helping build my future?
- Which liabilities are limiting my financial freedom?
- What is one asset I can begin investing in this year?

Then develop a plan to increase your assets while reducing unnecessary liabilities.

Reflection Questions

- Am I spending more money building assets or buying liabilities?

- What purchases have helped strengthen my financial future?
- What purchases have slowed my financial progress?
- What changes can I make to better steward the resources God has entrusted to me?

Biblical Wisdom

"The plans of the diligent lead to profit as surely as haste leads to poverty." — **Proverbs 21:5 (NIV)**

Wise financial decisions are rarely impulsive. Lasting wealth is built through patience, planning, and consistent stewardship.

Notes:

Chapter 6
The Power of Compounding

"Whoever can be trusted with very little can also be trusted with much..." — **Luke 16:10 (NIV)**

Vaughn and Yolanda's Principle

"Small, faithful investments made consistently over time often produce greater results than occasional large investments."

Little by Little Becomes Much

Many people underestimate the power of small beginnings.

They believe they must have thousands of dollars before they can begin investing. As a result, they postpone investing year after year, waiting for the "perfect time."

The truth is, the best time to begin building wealth is now.

One of the greatest financial principles is the power of compounding. Compounding occurs when your money earns money, and those earnings continue earning more money over time. Instead of simply saving, your investments begin to grow on both your original investment and the earnings they generate.

The longer your money remains invested, the greater the potential for growth.

Time Is Your Greatest Ally

Many people focus on how much money they need to invest.

Wise stewards understand that time is often more valuable than the amount invested.

Someone who consistently invests a modest amount over many years may accumulate significantly more wealth than someone who waits to invest a larger amount later in life.

- The lesson is simple:
- Start where you are.
- Start with what you have.
- Most importantly, start now.
- Consistency matters more than perfection.

The Blessing of Patience

Our culture celebrates immediate results.

Building wealth requires patience.

Just as a farmer plants a seed and waits for the harvest, investors must allow time for their money to grow.

Every contribution you make is another seed planted for your future.

Some seasons produce rapid growth.

Other seasons require patience.

Faithful stewardship means remaining committed regardless of market conditions or temporary setbacks.

Make Investing a Habit

One of the best ways to benefit from compounding is to invest consistently.

Instead of trying to predict the perfect time to invest, develop the habit of investing regularly.

Small monthly investments made over many years often produce remarkable results because they allow time and consistency to work together.

The amount is less important than the habit.

Building the discipline to invest regularly creates a foundation for long-term financial freedom.

Reinvest Your Earnings

Compounding becomes even more powerful when you allow your earnings to remain invested.

Instead of immediately spending dividends, interest, or investment gains, consider reinvesting them.

Each reinvestment increases your potential for future growth.

Over time, this cycle of earning and reinvesting can significantly strengthen your financial future.

Stewardship Challenge

If you are not currently investing, commit to taking the first step this month.

Open an investment account or increase your existing contributions, even if it is only a small amount.

If you already invest, review your plan and determine whether you can increase your monthly contribution.

Remember, consistency is more important than size.

Reflection Questions

- Have I delayed investing because I thought I needed more money?
- What small amount can I begin investing consistently?
- Am I allowing time to work in my favor?
- How can I make investing a regular financial habit?

Take a few moments to write your answers and identify one action you will take this week.

Biblical Wisdom

"Let us not become weary in doing good, for at the proper time we will reap a harvest if we do not give up."
— Galatians 6:9 (NIV)

While this verse speaks to perseverance in doing good, it also reminds us that faithful, consistent effort often produces results over time. In our financial lives, patience and discipline can lead to lasting rewards.

Notes:

Chapter 7
The 5-to-1 Ownership Rule
Become More Than a customer, Become an Owner

*"The plans of the diligent lead to profit as surely as haste leads to poverty."— **Proverbs 21:5 (NIV)***

Vaughn and Yolanda's Principle

"Whenever possible, don't just spend money with great companies look for opportunities to become an owner in them."

A Different Way of Thinking

Most people spend their entire lives helping businesses become successful.

- They shop at their favorite stores every week.
- They purchase products from companies they trust.
- They recommend those companies to family and friends.
- They contribute to the growth of businesses every day.

Yet many never stop to ask onc important question: **"Wliy am I only a customer when I could also become an owner?"**

The 5-to-1 Ownership Rule is a simple principle that encourages a shift in mindset from simply consuming to participating in the growth of businesses you believe in.

Understanding the 5-to-1 Ownership Rule

This principle is not a mathematical formula or a rule that must be followed exactly.

Instead, it is a reminder to think differently about your spending.

As a personal stewardship guideline, consider this:

For every five dollars you consistently spend with companies you know and trust, look for opportunities to invest one dollar in businesses you believe have long-term potential.

The goal is not to stop buying products.

The goal is to remember that ownership can create opportunities that spending alone cannot.

Think Like an Owner

When you become an owner, your perspective begins to change.

Instead of only asking,

"What can this company sell me?"

You begin asking,

"Is this a business that is serving people well and creating long-term value?"

Ownership encourages patience.

It encourages research.

It encourages long term thinking.

These are qualities that also strengthen wise stewardship.

Invest in Businesses You Know

One of the simplest ways to begin investing is by paying attention to the companies you already use.

Think about the businesses you support regularly.

Perhaps you shop at:

- Walmart
- Costco
- Apple
- Nike
- Starbucks

Or maybe there are other companies whose products and services have earned your trust.

If those businesses demonstrate strong leadership, provide products people continue to use, and have a history of serving customers well, they may be worth studying further as potential investments.

The key word is study.

Never invest simply because you like a product.

Learn how the company operates, how it earns money, and whether it aligns with your long-term financial goals.

Ownership Creates Opportunity

Owning even a small piece of a business changes your financial perspective.

You begin to understand that wealth is often created through ownership rather than consumption.

As businesses grow, they may increase in value or provide income through dividends, allowing your money to work alongside you.

While all investments involve risk and no investment is guaranteed, becoming an informed owner rather than only a consumer can open the door to long-term wealth building.

Stewardship Requires Wisdom

Wise stewardship means making thoughtful decisions with the resources God has entrusted to us.

Before investing, take time to:

- Learn about the business.
- Understand the risks.
- Invest within your financial means.
- Diversify rather than depending on a single investment.
- Focus on long-term growth rather than short-term speculation.

Ownership should never replace wisdom.

Instead, wisdom should guide every investment decision.

Stewardship Challenge

This week, make a list of five companies you regularly support.

Choose one of those companies and spend time learning about its business.

Ask yourself:

- What products or services does it provide?
- How does it earn money?
- Does it have a history of serving customers well?
- Is it a company I would feel comfortable owning?

Remember, the goal is not to invest immediately.

The goal is to begin thinking like an owner.

Reflection Questions

- Do I spend more time consuming than investing?
- Which companies do I support most often?
- Have I ever considered becoming an owner instead of only a customer?
- What can I learn about investing before making my first investment?

Biblical Wisdom

"Good planning and hard work lead to prosperity, but hasty shortcuts lead to poverty."— **Proverbs 21:5 (NLT)**

Wise stewardship involves careful planning, thoughtful research, and patience. Building wealth is rarely the result of quick decisions; it is the product of consistent, informed choices made over time.

Notes:______________________________________

Chapter 8
Invest in What You Understand

"The simple believe anything, but the prudent give thought to their steps." — Proverbs 14:15 (NIV)

Vaughn and Yolanda's Principle

"Never invest your money in something you do not understand. Wise stewardship begins with knowledge, patience, and careful decision-making."

Knowledge Builds Confidence

One of the biggest mistakes people make is investing based on emotions, rumors, or someone else's opinion.

A friend tells them about a "can't miss" investment.

A television personality recommends a stock.

Social media promises quick profits.

Without taking time to learn, many people invest their hard-earned money into opportunities they do not fully understand.

Wise stewardship requires something different.

It requires learning before investing.

God has given us the ability to think, study, and make sound decisions. Before committing our financial resources, we should seek understanding. Knowledge helps us make informed decisions and avoid unnecessary risks.

Learn Before You Invest

Every investment represents ownership in something.

Before investing, ask questions such as:

- What does this company or investment actually do?
- How does it generate income?
- Why do people buy its products or services?
- Does it solve a real problem?
- Do I understand the risks involved?

If you cannot clearly explain an investment to someone else, you may need to spend more time learning before committing your money.

There is wisdom in taking your time.

Pay Attention to Everyday Life

Many successful investments begin with careful observation.

Think about the products and services you use regularly.

Which businesses consistently provide value?

Which companies have earned your trust over time?

Which products do your family, friends, and community continue to purchase?

These observations can become the starting point for further research.

However, using a product does not automatically make it a good investment. It simply gives you a place to begin learning.

Don't Follow the Crowd

History has shown that excitement can cause people to make poor financial decisions.

When everyone seems to be rushing toward the same investment, emotions often replace wisdom.

Fear of missing out has caused many people to invest at the wrong time and suffer unnecessary losses.

A wise steward remains patient.

Instead of chasing trends, take time to research, ask questions, and make decisions based on knowledge rather than emotion.

Patience is often one of the greatest investments you can make.

Continue Learning

Investing is not something you master overnight.

The more you learn, the more confident you become.

Read books.

Attend financial workshops.

Ask questions.

Learn from trusted financial professionals.

Most importantly, never stop growing in knowledge.

Financial education is an investment that continues paying dividends throughout your life.

Stewardship Challenge

Choose one company, business, or investment that interests you.

Spend time this week learning about it.

Ask yourself:

- What products or services does it provide?
- How does it earn money?
- Why do customers continue to support it?
- What makes it successful?

Remember, your goal this week is not to invest.

Your goal is to become a better student of financial stewardship.

Reflection Questions

- Have I ever invested because someone else told me to?
- What investment do I currently own that I understand well?
- What financial topics do I need to learn more about?
- How can I continue growing in financial knowledge?

Take time to write your answers and commit to becoming a lifelong learner.

Biblical Wisdom

"The heart of the discerning acquires knowledge, for the ears of the wise seek it out."— **Proverbs 18:15 (NIV)**

God calls us to seek wisdom and understanding before making important decisions. Knowledge, combined with patience and discernment, helps us become faithful stewards of the resources He has entrusted to us.

Notes:

Chapter 9
Increase Your Income Streams

"You shall remember the Lord your God, for it is He who gives you the ability to produce wealth."— Deuteronomy 8:18 (NIV)

Vaughn and Yolanda's Principle

"God often provides more than one opportunity to prosper. Wise stewards recognize those opportunities and use them faithfully."

Don't Depend on One Source

Many people rely on a single paycheck to support their entire household.

While there is nothing wrong with earning a living through employment, depending on one source of income can leave a family financially vulnerable.

- Unexpected events happen.
- A company may downsize.
- A business may experience slower sales.
- An illness may interrupt your ability to work.

When all of your income comes from one source, unexpected changes can quickly create financial stress.

Wise stewards understand the value of developing additional sources of income over time.

God Gives Us Different Gifts

God has given each of us unique talents, skills, experiences, and abilities.

Some people are gifted teachers.

Others are skilled craftsmen, artists, writers, musicians, business owners, or problem solvers.

These gifts are more than talents they are opportunities.

Throughout Scripture, God calls His people to faithfully use what He has entrusted to them. When we develop our gifts and use them wisely, they often create opportunities to serve others while providing additional income.

Sometimes the greatest opportunity is already in your hands.

Examples of Income Streams

Additional income does not always require working another full-time job.

It may come through:

- Employment income
- A small business
- Rental property
- Dividend-paying investments
- Royalties from books or creative works
- Online sales
- Consulting or coaching
- Freelance services
- Speaking or teaching

Not every opportunity is right for every person.

The goal is to prayerfully consider how God has uniquely equipped you and use those gifts wisely.

Start with What You Have

Many people delay pursuing additional income because they believe they need more money, more education, or better circumstances.

Often, they already possess the skills they need to begin.

You may have knowledge that others are willing to learn.

You may have experience that can solve someone's problem.

You may have a hobby that can become a business.

Don't overlook the opportunities God has already placed before you.

Small beginnings often lead to greater opportunities.

Build Gradually

- Creating additional income streams takes time.
- You do not have to build everything at once.
- Start with one opportunity.
- Learn from the experience.
- Strengthen it before pursuing another.
- Growing steadily is often wiser than trying to do too much too quickly.
- Faithful stewardship values consistency over haste.

Stewardship Challenge

This week, make a list of your gifts, skills, experiences, and interests.

Ask yourself:

- What do I enjoy doing?
- What problems can I help solve?
- Is there a skill I could develop into additional income?
- What opportunity has God already placed before me?

Pray for wisdom and be open to opportunities that align with your gifts and values.

Reflection Questions

- Am I relying entirely on one source of income?
- What skills or talents have I overlooked?
- How can I use my gifts to serve others while strengthening my financial future?
- What is one practical step I can take this month toward creating an additional income stream?

Take time to write your answers and identify one opportunity you will begin exploring.

Biblical Wisdom

"Whatever you do, work at it with all your heart, as working for the Lord, not for human masters."
— Colossians 3:23 (NIV)

Whether you earn income through employment, business ownership, investing, or another opportunity, work with excellence, integrity, and a desire to honor God through faithful stewardship.

Notes:

Chapter 10
Make Money While You Sleep

"The blessing of the Lord brings wealth, without painful toil for it."
— Proverbs 10:22 (NIV)

Vaughn and Yolanda's Principle

"The goal is not to work harder for money your entire life. The goal is to build assets that continue working for you while you faithfully pursue God's purpose for your life."

The Ultimate Goal

Most people spend their lives trading time for money.

They wake up early, work long hours, receive a paycheck, pay their bills, and repeat the cycle week after week, year after year.

There is dignity in honest work, and God calls us to work faithfully. However, there is a difference between earning an income and achieving financial freedom.

If your income depends entirely on your ability to work every day, there will always be limits on your time, your opportunities, and your financial future.

Financial freedom begins when your money starts working alongside you.

Let Your Assets Produce Income

Throughout this book, we have discussed avoiding unnecessary debt, saving consistently, investing wisely, and purchasing assets instead of liabilities.

Those principles work together for one purpose—to build income-producing assets.

Assets have the potential to generate income whether you are working, spending time with your family, serving in your church, traveling, or enjoying retirement.

Examples include:

- Dividend paying investments
- Rental properties
- Businesses
- Books and publications
- Digital products
- Royalties
- Licensing agreements

These assets may require time and effort to build, but once established, they can continue producing income long after the initial work has been completed.

Build Today for Tomorrow

Many people spend every dollar they earn.

Wise stewards invest a portion of today's income to create tomorrow's opportunities.

Every investment you make is a step toward greater financial independence.

Every asset you acquire has the potential to strengthen your future.

Building wealth is not about becoming rich overnight.

It is about making consistent decisions that allow your resources to grow over time.

Financial Freedom Creates Options

Money alone does not create happiness. However, financial freedom creates choices.

- It allows you to spend more time with your family.
- It gives you the ability to serve others more generously.
- It provides flexibility during unexpected seasons of life.
- It reduces financial stress and allows you to make decisions based on wisdom rather than desperation.

The purpose of financial freedom is not to impress people. The purpose is to create opportunities to live, give, and serve more effectively.

Faithfulness Before Freedom

Financial freedom is rarely achieved through one great investment or one successful business.

More often, it is the result of years of faithful stewardship.

- Saving consistently.
- Living below your means.
- Avoiding unnecessary debt.
- Investing wisely.
- Remaining patient.

Small decisions repeated over many years often produce extraordinary results.

God honors faithfulness.

As we faithfully manage what He has entrusted to us, we become better prepared for greater opportunities and greater responsibility.

Stewardship Challenge

Take a few moments to think about your future.

Ask yourself:

- What assets am I building today?
- Which assets have the potential to generate income in the future?
- What is one income-producing asset I can begin working toward this year?

Develop one specific goal that moves you closer to financial freedom.

Then begin taking small, consistent steps toward achieving it.

Reflection Questions

- Does all of my income depend on my time?
- What assets am I currently building?
- How can I begin creating income that is not solely dependent on my daily work?
- What changes do I need to make to move closer to financial freedom?
- Write your answers and review them regularly as you continue building your financial future.

Biblical Wisdom

"Commit to the Lord whatever you do, and He will establish your plans." — **Proverbs 16:3 (NIV)**

As we seek financial freedom, our ultimate goal should be to honor God through faithful stewardship. When our plans are guided by wisdom, integrity, and dependence on Him, our work takes on greater purpose.

Notes:

Chapter 11
Master Delayed Gratification

"Better a patient person than a warrior, one with self-control than one who takes a city." — **Proverbs 16:32 (NIV)**

Vaughn and Yolanda's Principle

"Every time you choose wisdom over impulse, you invest in your future."

The Power of Waiting

We live in a world that encourages instant gratification.

We can order products with a few clicks and have them delivered within days. We can finance almost anything and walk away with it immediately. Advertisements constantly tell us that if we want something today, we shouldn't wait until tomorrow.

Unfortunately, this mindset often leads people into unnecessary debt and financial stress.

God's wisdom teaches a different approach.

Delayed gratification is the ability to wait for something better rather than settling for immediate satisfaction. It is choosing long-term financial freedom over short-term pleasure.

- Waiting is not weakness.
- Waiting is wisdom.

Self-Control Is a Financial Strength

The Bible teaches that self-control is a valuable character trait.

The same discipline that helps us grow spiritually also strengthens our financial lives.

When we practice self-control, we become less likely to make emotional purchases, take on unnecessary debt, or spend money without a plan.

Instead of reacting to every sale or impulse, we learn to pause, pray, and make thoughtful decisions.

Every wise financial decision strengthens the habit of self-control.

The Difference Between Wants and Timing

There is nothing wrong with wanting nice things.

God blesses us in many ways, and it is appropriate to enjoy His blessings.

The question is not whether something is good.

The question is whether **now** is the right time.

Many purchases become financial burdens simply because they were made too soon.

Sometimes waiting a few months allows you to save the money, avoid debt, or determine that you no longer want the item at all.

Good timing is part of wise stewardship.

Temporary Sacrifice, Lasting Reward

Many financially successful people share one common habit.

They are willing to sacrifice today for something greater tomorrow.

They may drive an older vehicle while investing for retirement.

They may delay upgrading their home while building an emergency fund.

They may choose to invest instead of spending every raise they receive.

These decisions may not always be easy, but they often lead to lasting financial freedom.

Temporary sacrifice creates opportunities that impulsive spending cannot.

Patience Produces Peace

One of the greatest rewards of delayed gratification is peace of mind.

When you save before you spend, avoid unnecessary debt, and make thoughtful financial decisions, you experience less stress and greater confidence.

Instead of wondering how you will make the next payment, you can enjoy what you own knowing it was purchased wisely.

Patience not only protects your finances it protects your peace.

Stewardship Challenge

Choose one purchase you have been considering.

Instead of buying it immediately, wait 30 days.

During that time:

- Pray for wisdom.
- Review your financial goals.
- Determine whether the purchase is still necessary.
- Save the money instead of spending it.

At the end of the 30 days, decide whether the purchase still aligns with your priorities.

You may discover that waiting gives you greater clarity.

Reflection Questions

- What purchases have I made because I acted too quickly?
- How has impatience affected my finances?
- What financial goal is worth waiting for?
- How can I practice greater self-control in my spending?

Take time to write your answers and identify one habit you will begin changing this week.

Biblical Wisdom

"A person without self-control is like a city with broken-down walls." — **Proverbs 25:28 (NLT)**

Self-control protects every area of our lives, including our finances. When we learn to control our spending, we strengthen our ability to build wealth, avoid unnecessary debt, and faithfully manage the resources God has entrusted to us.

Notes:

Chapter 12
Protect What You Build

"The prudent see danger and take refuge, but the simple keep going and pay the penalty." — **Proverbs 22:3 (NIV)**

Vaughn and Yolanda's Principle

"Building wealth is an act of stewardship. Protecting it is an act of wisdom."

Faithful Stewards Think Ahead

Throughout this book, we have focused on building a strong financial foundation.

We have learned the importance of living within our means, avoiding unnecessary debt, saving consistently, investing wisely, and creating opportunities for financial freedom.

These principles help us build wealth.

However, faithful stewardship does not end when wealth is created.

Wise stewards also take steps to protect what God has entrusted to them.

Protecting your finances is not about living in fear. It is about planning wisely so that unexpected events do not undo years of faithful stewardship.

Protect Your Family

One of the greatest responsibilities we have is caring for those God has entrusted to us.

While no one likes to think about illness, accidents, disability, or death, preparing for these possibilities is an expression of love and responsibility.

Protection begins with asking simple questions:

- If something happened to me tomorrow, would my family be financially prepared?
- Have I made plans that would reduce confusion during difficult times?
- Am I protecting the resources God has entrusted to my care?

Planning ahead provides peace of mind for both you and those you love.

Use Wisdom in Managing Risk

- Life is unpredictable.
- Storms happen.
- Accidents occur.
- Health challenges arise.
- Markets change.

These realities remind us why preparation matters.

Wise financial stewardship includes reducing unnecessary risk whenever possible.

This may include maintaining appropriate insurance coverage, building an emergency fund, avoiding excessive debt, diversifying investments, and regularly reviewing your financial plans.

Preparing wisely allows you to respond with confidence rather than panic when unexpected challenges arise.

Build a Legacy, Not Just Wealth

Financial freedom is not measured only by what you accumulate.

It is also measured by what you leave behind.

A lasting legacy includes more than money.

- It includes faith.
- Character.
- Wisdom.
- Generosity.
- Integrity.

As you build wealth, think about how your financial decisions today will impact future generations.

Teach your children and grandchildren the value of hard work, saving, giving, investing, and faithful stewardship.

Passing down financial wisdom is one of the greatest gifts you can leave your family.

Continue Growing

Financial stewardship is a lifelong journey.

- Laws change.
- Markets change.
- Life circumstances change.

- Continue learning.
- Seek wise counsel.
- Review your financial plans regularly.
- Remain teachable.

The more you grow in knowledge and wisdom, the better prepared you will be to manage the opportunities God places before you.

Stewardship Challenge

Take time this week to review your financial protection plan.

Ask yourself:

- Do I have an emergency fund?
- Is my insurance coverage adequate?
- Have I prepared a will or estate plan?
- Have I discussed my financial wishes with my family?
- What one step can I take this month to better protect what God has entrusted to me?

Write down one action you will complete within the next 30 days.

Reflection Questions

- Have I spent more time building wealth than protecting it?
- What financial risks concern me the most?
- What steps can I take to better prepare my family for the future?
- How do I want my financial legacy to be remembered?

Take time to write your answers and discuss them with your family if appropriate.

Biblical Wisdom

"A good person leaves an inheritance for their children's children..." — **Proverbs 13:22 (NIV)**

An inheritance is more than money. It is the legacy of wisdom, faithful stewardship, generosity, and preparation that blesses future generations.

Notes:

Conclusion

A Foundation for Financial Freedom

As we conclude this section, I want to leave you with one simple truth:

Financial freedom begins with faithful stewardship.

Throughout these chapters, we've explored biblical principles that can transform the way you think about money. We learned the importance of living within our means, avoiding unnecessary debt, building savings, investing wisely, creating multiple streams of income, practicing patience, and protecting what God has entrusted to us.

These are not just financial principles they are biblical principles of stewardship.

God calls us to faithfully manage our resources with wisdom, discipline, integrity, and generosity. Financial freedom is not about becoming wealthy for wealth's sake. It is about creating the freedom to provide for your family, serve others, give generously, and fulfill God's purpose for your life.

Remember, lasting wealth is not built through one big decision. It is built through small, wise decisions made consistently over time.

Our prayer is that these principles become more than something you read they become a way of life.

- Faith provides the foundation.
- Wisdom guides the journey.
- Stewardship builds the legacy.

May God bless you as you continue your journey toward financial freedom.

Vaughn and Yolanda Cowan

www.ingramcontent.com/pod-product-compliance
Lightning Source LLC
LaVergne TN
LVHW102228300926
849160LV00005B/68
* 9 7 8 0 9 6 0 1 0 8 1 7 6 *